Cryptocurrency

Learn The Foundations, Technologies, And Investment
Strategies Necessary To Succeed In The World Of Digital
Currency

*(Unlocking The Digital Frontier: A Step By Step Guide To
Investing In Cryptocurrencies)*

TorstenHöfler

TABLE OF CONTENT

Introduction

We are grateful that you have decided to purchase and download our book, Cryptocurrency: A Clear and Simple Guide to Understand and Master Cryptocurrency. You will get a comprehensive guide to all you need to know about becoming engaged in the cryptocurrency market inside the pages of this book. Even if you are not interested in trading or investing, this work will equip you with sufficient knowledge to explain the topic to your colleagues, produce books and articles about cryptocurrency, and grasp this innovative and fascinating technology on a more fundamental level. This book will cover a wide variety of subjects, and each subject will have its own section (or chapter) that has seven chapters.

This book will go through the most important ones in great depth, and there is a wealth of material available on cryptocurrencies. The following are some of the topics that will be covered: defining the invention of cryptocurrency, explaining the underlying mechanics behind cryptocurrency, exploring the history of cryptocurrency, reviewing all of the new and upcoming applications of the technology, providing a primer on getting involved with trading and investing in cryptocoins, discussing the legal concerns that face cryptocurrency, and finally discussing the security risks that are associated with cryptocurrency. In each chapter, there is a portion that serves as an introduction and describes what will be addressed, as well as a section that serves as a conclusion and summarizes all of the significant themes that were discussed in that chapter.

We have high hopes that you will find this book to be a useful and comprehensive resource covering all aspects of cryptocurrencies. Once again, I want to thank you for taking the time to read this article, and I wish you the best of success in your future endeavors trading and investing in cryptocurrencies and cryptocoins.

What Exactly Is Meant By "Technical Analysis"?

The development of charting packages and trading platforms has contributed, at least in part, to the rise in popularity of technical analysis as a method of trading. This popularity is expected to continue unabated. In any event, for a trader who is just starting out, learning how to use technical analysis and how it may help you anticipate trends in the market can be an extremely challenging and intimidating task.

The examination of price movements in a market is known as technical analysis, and it is a method through which traders make use of striking chart patterns and indicators to anticipate future patterns on the watch. It is a graphical depiction of the execution of a market at various intervals during the day. Before initiating a trade, the investor is given the opportunity to make use of this data as price action, indications, and examples to guide and educate future pattern formation.

You will get familiar with the fundamentals of this trading strategy and learn how it may be used to trade in the financial markets by reading this article, which is titled Technical Analysis for Beginners.

Acquiring Knowledge of Technical Analysis

Understanding specific instances from charts is a necessary part of doing technical analysis. Traders make use of significant information considering price and volume, and they employ this data to differentiate trading opportunities based on simple instances on the lookout. Traders utilize a variety of indicators to apply to charts in order to determine section and depart foci for the purpose of increasing a trade's potential while maintaining high risk to reward ratios.

An sample of a diagram that makes use of the MACD and RSI indicators is shown in the chart that can be seen beneath.

Traders who use technical analysis acknowledge that changes in financial factors are the major drivers of price movements in the market; nonetheless, they continue to monitor price patterns from the past in the hopes of better predicting how prices will change in the future. Even if these methods of communication might fluctuate, it can be quite important to grasp the differences between primary analysis and technical analysis as well as how to combine the two.

Research that brings together the primary findings and the technical analyses.

What Factors Contribute To A Cryptocurrency's Value?

The prices of cryptocurrencies are influenced by a wide variety of variables. However, the variables that have the most significant impact on it are those that are associated with the mood of the market. These components are as follows:

Forks - A fork is a divide or production of new tokens from an existing one (for example, Bitcoin Cash or Bitcoin Gold from Bitcoins). Forks are a highly perilous occurrence for cryptocurrency traders, whether they are seasoned pros or just starting out. In most cases, the impacted cryptocurrency will come under pressure in the days leading up to the event as well as in the days immediately after it. When something like this occurs, the value of the coin itself suffers to a significant degree.

Changes in the underlying network and technology Becausecryptocurrencies are representations of the underlying network and technology, any changes to those two factors (such as upgrades or alterations) will have an effect on the price of the coin. On the other hand, the price of the cryptocurrency almost never goes down, which is a benefit for those who already own some of it since it tends to go up. The majority of traders who are looking for a quick profit often sell their coins one day after a significant technological upgrade has taken place.

rules - Cryptocurrencies are also impacted by rules, particularly the ones that are created by the country's government, as well as news that is connected to the changes in the cryptocurrency's policy. For instance, if the government of a particular nation makes the decision to pass laws that restrict the use of bitcoins inside its borders, the price of bitcoins in that country will be impacted as a direct result of these new rules.

Market Sentiment: There is nothing steady or permanent when it comes to market sentiment, regardless of how powerful the market or the cryptocurrency may be. Because individuals are still motivated by their feelings, it will still have an impact on the trading choices they make. A rally that took place three years ago, when some people claimed that the year itself marked the beginning of the crypto age and gave birth to several different cryptocurrencies, is an excellent illustration of what I mean. One year later, however, these same individuals believed that it is still too early for cryptocurrencies to take over the economy, which resulted in the largest selling of bitcoin in the history of the world.

Trading Strategies That Are Used Most Often With Bitcoin and Other Cryptocurrencies

When it comes to trading cryptocurrencies, there is no such thing as a Holy Grail or a foolproof method just as there is no such thing with any other kind of investment. However, despite the fact that putting in a lot of effort and spending a lot of time in front of your charts, this will only increase the likelihood of your being successful while trading cryptocurrencies. However, there are already widely accepted trading techniques that were developed, tried and proven by veteran crypto traders. These strategies may be used to trade Bitcoin and other cryptocurrencies. The following is a list of some of them:

Trading with Cryptocurrencies Using Swings

The trading technique known as swing trading is characterized by short-term investments and has shown to be an efficient method for generating gains from the trends and lengthy fluctuations of cryptocurrency markets. Because the most recent trend is your ally, swing trading involves taking positions that might last anywhere from two days to two weeks, depending on the level of excitement around the coin in question. It is also possible to sustain positions over a period of months, although in most cases this does not occur.

Trading cryptocurrencies on a daily basis

Day trading is a trading technique that includes creating long and short positions within a day, then closing those positions or executing a transaction during the same day. This method gets its name from the fact that it involves opening long and short positions within a day. You are free to continue using a variety of time frames, but the primary trait of your trading technique is that your deals do not remain open for more than a few hours at a time.

When engaging in day trading, it is important to keep an eye on the volatility of the underlying cryptocurrency as well as short-term price movements such as scalping, reversals, and breakouts. Taking this course of action could result in a larger reward for you, but it might also include more risky wagers on your part.

Long-Term Developments in Cryptocurrency

The vast majority of the movements associated with trading cryptocurrencies are volatile, which means that there is no actual guarantee that the market as a whole will triumph over the course of the years. Because cryptocurrency traders, brokers, and the sector as a whole are still in the early stages of growth, many industry professionals do not engage in long-term cryptocurrency trading. The only people who really invest, on the other hand, are those who have faith in the potential benefits offered by blockchain technology and cryptocurrency.

Long-term trading methods in cryptocurrencies entail following trends that continue to develop on larger periods such as daily, weekly, and monthly charts. Examples of these charts include Bitcoin and Ethereum. Technical indicators like as moving averages, divergences, and volume may tell you if the current trend is coming to an end and a new one is beginning, but this depends on the development that is taking place.

What Role Does Blockchain Play In The World Of Digital Currency?

The technology known as blockchain makes it possible for a decentralized digital currency to function without the need for a central bank. One of the numerous applications that may take use of the advantages offered by decentralization in the digital world is currency trading, which can take place on a distributed ledger known as a blockchain.

Because it is secured by cryptography, the money stored on a blockchain is referred to as cryptocurrency.

WHAT DOES IT MEAN TO USE A CRYPTOCURRENCY?

In a decentralized community that uses a cryptocurrency, any rule or regulation may be written into the cryptographic algorithm that regulates the community. This algorithm governs the cryptocurrency. The term "cryptocurrency" refers to any digital asset that is secured using cryptography and traded using a currency. This refers to a money that is essentially backed by cryptography and is also rendered uncommon by the use of encryption.

WORTH NOTING

The encryption that underpins a cryptocurrency is where trust in that coin originates. Because this is a novel idea, when compared to the thousands of years that have been spent using precious metals, it will take some time before an increasing number of people begin to comprehend the genuine advantages that come with the new system.

The Differences Between Day Trading and Swing Trading in Chapter Three

The time frame that a trader choose to trade on may have a considerable impact on both the trading system and the gain obtained from it. Swing traders enter and exit transactions over the course of many days, weeks, or even months, in contrast to day traders, who initiate and shut a number of positions during the span of a single trading day. These two distinct trading strategies may be suitable for various brokers depending on the amount of cash available, the amount of time available, the level of brain science required, and the market that is being traded.

It is not possible to rank one trading method above another; rather, a trader's success should be determined by the method that is most suited to their local market circumstances. Some brokers choose to engage in any one of these strategies, while others may engage in day trading, swing trading, and buy-and-hold investing all at the same time.

The Difference Between Day Trading And Swing Trading

Possibilities of Gains

Day trading is attractive to investors who are looking for a quick increase in their earnings. Assume that a broker puts up a risk of 0.5 percent of their total capital on each trade. In the case that they are unsuccessful, they will incur a loss of 0.5%; but, if they are successful, they will generate 1% in profit (a reward to risk ratio of 2:1).

In addition, let's suppose that they are successful in fifty percent of their deals. If they make six transactions each day, they will, on average, add around 1.5% to their record amount each day, minus any trading charges they incur. This is assuming that they do not incur any trading losses. A trading account may expand by more than 200% over the year if it earned at least 1% every day, even without compounding the earnings.

On the other hand, despite the fact that recreating those statistics and achieving those returns seems to be anything but tough, the reality is that nothing is ever so straightforward. It won't come easy if you want to make twice as much on wins as you lost on failures, while also winning half of the large number of deals you embark on. Day trading has the opportunity for speedy profits, but it also presents the danger of your trading account being wiped out in a hurry.

The gains and losses from swing trading are accumulated over a longer period of time than those from day trading. However, there are some swing trades that have the potential to quickly bring about huge wins or losses for the trader. Let's say a swing trader follows the same criteria for risk management and bets 0.5% of their total capital on each transaction in the hopes of achieving a return of 1% to 2% on the successful trades they execute.

Assume they earn 1.5% on average on winning exchanges and lose 0.5% on trades when they come out on the losing end. They participate in six trades every month, of which they are successful in three of those trades. The potential profit for a swing trader in a typical month is three percent of the account balance, less any fees or commissions paid. That works out to roughly 36% over the course of the year, which is an impressive number; nevertheless, it has less potential than the possible profit that may be made by day traders.

The distinction between the two trading strategies may be better understood with the help of these illustrative scenarios. Changing factors like as the number of transactions, the average win compared to the average loss, or the number of trades won will unquestionably have an effect on the purchasing potential of a method.

When there is uncertainty, day trading has the potential to generate larger profits, at least on smaller balances. When the size of an account grows, it becomes more difficult to spend all of the available money profitably on day transactions that are very short-lived.

Day traders could find that the more cash they have, the lower the rate of return on their investments becomes. Their dollar returns might, in any event, increase higher, given that earning 5%

on $1 million is much more than earning 20% on $100,000, and that the former compares well to the latter. Swing traders have a lower chance of experiencing this kind of event.

Comparing Trading With Investing

Now that you understand the fundamentals of any cryptocurrency and how (simple) it is to purchase it with traditional money, the most important question that arises is: what are you going to do with it? After hearing so much about Bitcoin and other forms of digital money, you may finally have some of your very own; nevertheless, you may be wondering when the profits will start coming in.

The unfortunate truth is that it does not work in this case. At the very least, it does not in the sense of an investment that one can make and then forget about; the only time that the cryptocurrency may, in broad terms, earn money is when it is traded in for something else. If such is not the case, then it is only an asset whose value is shifting as a direct result of the generally dynamic market.

Bitcoin and other cryptocurrencies do not provide dividends. As long as you maintain it in its current shape, it will not make you any money and it will not cost you any money either. A single Bitcoin may be worth $2,000 or $20,000, but it doesn't become worth either of those amounts until it is sold or exchanged. It is similar to the Schrodinger's cat experiment, which is a phrase that has been overused but which I believe is appropriate in this context. As long as it continues to exist in crypto form, its direct worth will be more difficult to determine. There are still certain locations where products and services may be purchased with bitcoin, however because to the increased volatility, these locations are getting fewer and farther between. This portrayal of the worth of cryptocurrencies may be seen as problematic by bitcoin purists; yet, when viewed from the point of view of an everyday, first-time investor, this notion is accurate.

So, what can you do with the money you get from investing in cryptocurrency? First, let's take a look at the alternative that is more difficult but also potentially more lucrative: beginning to trade with it. This is a variant on the procedure that is already well-known via activities such as trading on the foreign exchange market or the commodity markets. You are familiar with the routine: purchase cheap and sell high, take your profit, and then wash and repeat. You star in your own reenactment of the film Wall Street, in which you play the roles of both Bud Fox and Gordon Gekko. The notions of a typical stockbroker are employed by cryptocurrency traders just as often as they are used in any other of the more traditional markets. The only real difference is that rather than stocks, you deal with various cryptocurrencies and the fluctuating prices of those coins.

Anyone who wishes to get into the crypto trading industry should exercise extreme care. You have to realize that by going through with this method, you are really giving yourself the opportunity to get an extra part-time employment. Between the several trading sessions, it is possible to trade while acting in a very carefree and disinterested manner; nevertheless, experience suggests that this is seldom the case. Instead, the majority of the time, you will place your investment on a cryptocurrency exchange and then start following the movement of the price of the cryptocurrency. You start trading, which means that you attempt to purchase on the downward swings of the price change and then dump (sell) once the price rebounds back up to its original level. You make a profit with each transaction such as this one, which you have the option to cash out or reinvest.

This may seem to be an acceptable practice at first glance, particularly taking into consideration that the majority of exchange platforms make use of auto-trading functions. This implies that you choose the quantity that you want to sell or acquire as well as the price level at which you desire for this to take place. When the price hits that level, the trade is automatically handled by the platform you use to access the exchange. However, if you start to engage in trading on a more regular basis, you will quickly realize that doing so requires a significant amount of both time and effort. You should familiarize yourself with the price estimates, the events that could influence the trading of a certain cryptocurrency, and a great deal more information before engaging in cryptocurrency trading. You may begin with Bitcoin, but you could also diversify into Ether, and then, after a few months, you might contemplate investing in a cryptocurrency that did not even exist a year ago. You will discover that you are looking at candlestick graphs an increasing amount, which is a sign that your mindset is shifting toward that of a stockbroker. I say this because this is how things operate in a large number of circumstances - being a trader implies just that - doing this as a full-time activity. The reason I say this is because this is how things function in a large number of cases. In the event that you do not experience an instant loss and begin to see the consequences of your trades, there is a good probability that you will desire more of the same activity. This is the point at which the spiral begins.

It is possible that you may be inclined to believe that your situation will be unique. If you were working on the cryptocurrency market full-time, you would believe that you would be able to avoid being sucked down the rabbit hole of becoming involved in it. Despite this, you would still be spending your time at a massive gambling establishment. Regrettably, even the most knowledgeable and experienced traders make errors and end up losing a significant amount of money. The issue with you is that, unlike experienced stockbrokers, you will not be trading other people's money but rather your own. Instead, you will be gambling with the money you have available to you. If you wish to spend some time each day on your trading sessions, this is an acceptable option for you. There is, however, a more effective method of investing in bitcoin that does not need you to take an active role in the process. This strategy, known as HODL, reduces the impact of some of the dangers described above while at the same time releasing the investor from the shackles of being chained to the price charts depicting red and green bars.

Why Should You Invest In Trading Cryptocurrencies?

According to the definition provided by the World Bank, an astonishingly large number of individuals are surviving their lives below the international standard for poverty. This demonstrates that the benefits and supports that contribute to the growth of the economy are divided in an unfair manner across the many nations and areas. According to Prahalad and Hammond (2002), some regions are now seeing the onset of economic anarchy, civil conflict, the breakdown of governance, and pestilence. In addition, economic reasons, such as limited access to financial services (Beck &Demirguc-Kunt, 2006) and rising inflation rates (Aisen&Veiga, 2006), are the primary contributors to poverty. In addition, research has shown that a lack of trust (Barham, Boadway, Marchand, &Pestieau, 1995) and corrupt government institutions are detrimental to economic growth (Olken, 2006).

As a medium to sustain the development process in developing countries by expanding financial inclusion, delivering better traceability of funds, and enabling people to escape poverty (Ammous, 2015), cryptocurrencies could provide a significant benefit by overcoming the lack of social trust and by raising the entry to financial services (Nakamoto, 2008). Cryptocurrencies could also provide a substantial advantage by overcoming the lack of social trust and by raising the entry to financial services.

Before we go on to an overview of cryptocurrencies and how they are being used in developing nations, we need to understand the benefits and drawbacks of cryptocurrencies offered for consumers in comparison to the central bank-issued fiat currencies, which are currencies that are completely standardized and are the same as the euro or the dollar. Not only that, but they purposefully emerged from the underlying technology as well. Blockchain technology is used by the majority of cryptocurrencies for their internal workings. The blocks that make up blockchain are scattered among the many nodes that make up the network. Blocks are used as the primary data storage mechanism for the blockchain's individual entries.

Bitcoin was the world's first ever kind of digital money to ever be created. Bitcoin was the world's first ever digital money to operate according to an algorithm. A decentralized peer-to-peer network will record and keep a record of all of the transactions that take place on the network. These transactions are visible to and may be monitored by all of the members of the network. Bitcoin's total market capitalization now exceeds $189 billion.

Bitcoin was first conceived upon and developed by Satoshi Nakamoto. In the year 2008, he released his white paper titled "Bitcoin: A Peer-to-Peer Electronic Cash System" (Nakamoto, 2008), which is considered to be the year that he developed bitcoin.

Ethereum is a distributed computing platform that uses open-source software. The distributed ledger technology known as blockchain underpins Ethereum. Additionally, it functions as a computer platform for the execution of smart contracts. In addition to this, it supports the updated version of the consensus method that Satoshi Nakamoto developed. The cryptocurrency known as Ether serves as the fuel that keeps the Ethereumblockchain network operational. Following in the footsteps of bitcoin as the most valuable and widely used cryptocurrency is ether. It is now valued at $18 billion on the market.

IN DEVELOPING COUNTRIES, THERE ARE OPPORTUNITIES TO BE FOUND IN CRYPTOCURRENCIES.

According to the findings of an inquiry into the economic challenges faced by emerging nations, cryptocurrencies have the potential to speed up the growth of a number of different industries. According to Chudnovsky and Lopez (2006), this theory proposes that innovations are useful strategic solutions for the process of emerging countries catching up to more developed nations.

People must have access to the internet in order to take advantage of the opportunities presented by the developments brought forth by crypto. That individuals who do not have access to the internet cannot engage in the trading of cryptocurrencies implies that others who do have internet access may do so. It has been observed that the use of the internet in developing nations has vastly improved over the course of the previous decade (Aker &Mbiti, 2010; Tapscott&Tapscott, 2016). This may be attributed to the fact that more people now have access to the internet.

Since there are no cryptocurrencies, the fiat money has to be converted into other currencies that are more frequently used, such as the United States Dollar or the Euro. After that, it has to be remade into the currency of the economy that is now in use. As a consequence of this, the vast majority of the time there is no liquid market that can be used to convert the local currency or the fiat currency being sought for the target currency. Using crypto currencies to optimize this situation is something that might be done. According to Ammous (2015), it would help the process go more quickly and at a lower cost.

Take for instance a person of Indian descent who lives and works in Chicago. This worker may send money to his family in India by using a local service provider that transforms US Dollars into Bitcoins. The worker's family lives in

India. The family may redeem their Bitcoins for rupees at a neighborhood service provider that offers the currency conversion service. Because of this procedure, businesses like Western Union end up being unable to function properly. In order to make the most of Bitcoin's potential, it is still necessary to create a liquid market that allows for the exchange of Bitcoin for both US dollars and Indian rupees. A number of new businesses have recently emerged with the exclusive objective of making the market for bitcoins more liquid. For example, BitPesa was first introduced to the public in Kenya. BitPesa makes liquid markets available for some particular currency channels, such as the direct conversion of Kenyan Shilling to US Dollars, for example.

Without needing a bank account, one may participate in international commerce via the use of cryptocurrencies. Bitcoin is a kind of cryptocurrency that has the potential to make it easier for people and companies to participate in international commerce on a local or regional scale. These companies and people have the ability to utilize Bitcoins as a form of exchange for purchasing things. This makes it easier to circumvent conventional online commerce systems (Scott, 2016), such as those that require the creation of a bank account.

By employing cryptocurrencies, developing nations may be able to better their current financial status, which indicates that cryptocurrencies may be able to assist developing countries in functioning as a substitute for traditional bank accounts. This is due to the fact that a Bitcoin wallet may be downloaded by anybody who has a computer and access to the internet (Honohan, 2008). Bitcoin wallets may function in a manner similar to that of bank accounts. People are able to manage their day-to-day finances, including their savings, there (Scott, 2016).

The significant expenditures that must be incurred by the transactions may serve to boost the chances of obtaining microcredits. This occurs at the price of a reduction in the expenses associated with transactions. If these expenses were eliminated, there is a very good possibility that there would be an increase in foreign finance. The use of cryptocurrencies makes it feasible for individuals in rich nations to transfer money to those living in poor countries.

This is made possible by the use of cryptocurrencies. Due to the nature of these transactions, the amounts involved would be very little, but the effects they may have on a person's life in a developing nation could be significant.

At this time, transactions involving microfinance might cost a significant amount of money due to the fact that they involve borrowing money and then returning it, both of which are subject to substantial trade costs. Sometimes the transaction charge is equal to or more than the amount of money being sent. On the other hand, if transaction costs are significantly reduced or totally ignored, this may increase the demand for loans, which in turn may lead to the expansion of the availability of such financing (Ammous, 2015).

Additionally, the combination of cryptocurrencies and smart contracts has the potential to become a defining element in the consolidation of societal trust as well as the combating of corruption via the implementation of a system that is more transparent. Ordinary people would be able to access the data of the cryptocurrency, which would be made available to the public on the blockchain. This would make it possible for them to monitor the use of the cash provided by the state. The government would also be able to track and manage the overall spending of their money, which would allow them to determine how they can enhance their budget provisioning as well as track and monitor the total expenditure of their money. -- Schmidt 2017 work by Kai Uwe).

next an examination of the relevant literature, the next discussion will concentrate on qualitative research that is based on interviews with industry professionals. In order to find an interview partner, social networking sites such as Xing and LinkedIn were used. The information and the expertise held by the many professionals who are contributing to this project are vastly different. They could be lecturers or ambassadors for consulting firms, or they might represent a startup as a company representative. The fact that they are located in various parts of the world is yet another factor that sets them apart from one another. They are quite different from one another in significant ways according to the place in which they live and work. Appendix B contains a summary of this information for your convenience.

Money In Us Dollars And Bitcoins

Are Bitcoins and fiat currency two names for the same thing? In this chapter, let us make an attempt at answering this question.

Lionel Trilling once said that despite the fact that humans are responsible for the creation of money and are the ones who utilize it, they do not really comprehend it. It is not possible to exert any control over it since it is governed by its own rules and has a life of its own.

Those who have a firm grasp of the inner-workings of monetary systems will find that the solution to the issue presented previously comes to them like a flash of lightning. Continue reading if you are one of the many people who are still struggling to comprehend all that has been said. Is it true that there is no such thing as having too much information?

You are in for a big surprise if the extent of your knowledge of money extends no farther than the fact that it may be found in either paper or coin form and that you have a strong affection for either.

Let us begin by altering your view of paper cash so that it better reflects reality. The term "fiat money" refers to any and all forms of currency. You may be wondering who exactly is in charge of deciding how much it is worth. However, we are the ones who are to blame for this. A very long time ago, there was not much of a distinction between traditional cash and the digital currency known as bitcoin.

At this point in history, the United States dollar and many other currencies throughout the world were still pegged to gold as their primary commodity of value. The Gold Standard was a commodity-based monetary system, and its guiding premise was that each dollar or unit of currency in circulation should be backed up by a predetermined quantity of gold bullion (the commodity) that would be stored in a reserve. The Gold Standard was a commodity-based monetary system.

You may be asking who exactly determined how much all of this gold is really worth at this point. The response, once again, is going to be "we did." This meant that the power we had previously

49

possessed was no longer available to us. The fact that the majority of people were unaware that this event had happened is maybe the saddest aspect of the whole situation.

There was a period of time when the Gold Standard was associated with a significant amount of debate as well as suspicion. It wasn't until the 1970s that it was discovered that there were more dollars in circulation all over the world than there was gold stored at Fort Knox to back the money. This revelation came about as a result of a comparison between the two locations.

At this point, the government of the United States of America made the decision to abandon the monetary standard. The United States served as a model for other nations to follow. You need to rethink your beliefs if you are one of the many people who still assume that Fort Knox guarantees the value of your currency. That is not the case, and it has not been the case for over forty years. This is a positive development in a number of respects.

The present situation at Fort Knox is fraught with a great deal of debate. various people believe there are conspiracies around the quantity of gold that is really housed at this facility; as a result, the general public is extremely concerned about the health of the United States dollar. It is considered to be the largest facility storing gold; nevertheless, there are various hypotheses about the amount of gold that is actually held in this facility.

If you now realize that the dollars you are carrying around are nothing more than a piece of paper representing monetary value and not a promissory note backed by gold, you will undoubtedly begin to form more favorable opinions on Bitcoin.

It shouldn't be too difficult for you to comprehend, in light of the fact that there is no commodity-based paper money, that fiat currency and Bitcoin aren't that unlike to one another, with the exception of one significant distinction between the two.

At their fundamental foundation, fiat currencies and bitcoin have a lot of similarities. However, it's not quite as straightforward as that. Bitcoins have a single distinguishing feature that makes them more enticing and promising.

The primary distinction between Bitcoin and other forms of money is that Bitcoin is a cryptocurrency. Cryptocurrency, in contrast to traditional currencies such as paper money, is a digital means of trade. It is the first of its type, and it is perhaps the only kind of global money that is not subject to any sort of meddling from governments or regulators.

There is some method behind the valuation of monetary units. A price tag has been put on it by the governing authority of the whole planet. The value of most of these items is derived from the United States dollar, and the current global standard contributes to the process of establishing the value of all other currencies.

Since the United States economy is often regarded as the most powerful in the world, its currency, the USD, is seen to be very robust. Because of this, the value of its currency is affected by many worldwide impressions of the states and the events taking place in those states, such as wars, the balance of trade, the credit balance, the reputation of the country's president, policies, taxes, laws, and expenditures, among other things.

The United States dollar, sometimes known as the "global currency standard," is driven less by the underlying commodities that it trades against and more by the public's perception of the value of the currency. In point of fact, it is nothing more than a kind of fiat money and nothing more. You should have understood by now that there is a significant gap between Bitcoin and fiat money since you have reached this point.

Bitcoin is a symbol of hope that one day we will be able to reclaim the Gold Standard, which was taken away from us in the 1970s. Bitcoin is a decentralized digital currency. Although it functions as a sort of fiat money, this is in actuality a decentralized peer-to-peer financial system.

You will have complete say over the amount of money that it is genuinely worth. Considering that bitcoins now have no established market value, you may be questioning whether it's a good idea to buy or use them at all. Bitcoin were once priced at around $13 per coin when they were first introduced in the year 2013, but their value has since skyrocketed to approximately $550 per coin. In November of 2013, the price of these coins was one thousand two hundred dollars.

The value of these coins is subject to a great deal of fluctuation. Because there is a limit on the total number of coins that may be produced, there is a very low probability that inflation would erode their value. When you give it some thought, the future might be seen to be rather intriguing. You are under no need to make a purchase of bitcoins right now if you are still unsure about the digital currency.

They did enjoy a really good year in 2013, but their performance is notoriously unpredictable. The next chapter will provide you with further information on Bitcoins.

Opportunities for Employment Regarding Bitcoin

There is a possibility for you to make money with the use of bitcoin. People who are self-employed have the opportunity to make money via the many occupations that are tied to bitcoin. One of the many ways you may earn bitcoins is by providing an online service, and if you want to pay for that service with bitcoins, all you have to do is add the address of your bitcoin wallet to the site where you are purchasing the service. There are a variety of websites and employment boards that are available to individuals that deal with digital currency.

Cryptogrind is a platform that assists in bringing together individuals looking for work and businesses that may be interested in hiring them in one location.

On the Coinality website, you may see listings for available jobs. Offers of employment on a freelance, part-time, and full-time basis. These are the types of occupations that pay in bitcoin in addition to other cryptocurrencies like Dogecoin and Litecoin.

BitGigsBitwage is a service that enables you to change a predetermined portion of your job income into bitcoin at your discretion. This message will be sent to the bitcoin address you provided.

A Guide to Purchasing Bitcoin

The vast majority of individuals believe that using digital money will become the norm in the near future. People that deal in bitcoins see this service as a payment system that can process transactions anywhere in the world more quickly and at a lower cost. Due to the fact that it is not backed by any government or a single financial institution, cryptocurrency may be exchanged for any kind of fiat money. In point of fact, the exchange rate of cryptocurrencies versus the dollar is something that attracts the attention of potential investors and traders. It is often cited as a primary factor in the development of digital currencies like bitcoin, and it is considered to be of essential importance. These cryptocurrencies may be used as an alternate form of payment alongside national fiat currency and conventional commodities such as gold.

The Internal Revenue Service (IRS) issued a statement in March 2014 stating that digital currencies such as bitcoin, Ether, and other similar cryptocurrencies are to be taxed as property and not as a currency. Every conceivable kind of transaction that takes place with bitcoins or any other digital currency will be subject to taxation. Whether via the mining of bitcoins or the purchase of them from another party.

The strategy of buying low and selling high is one that can be applied to bitcoin, just as it can to other assets. Increasing your currency by purchasing bitcoins via an exchange may be a very effective strategy for doing so. On the other hand, acquiring bitcoins may also be accomplished in a great number of different methods.

How Does The Bitcoin System Function?

In the last chapter, we discussed what Bitcoin is as well as some of its essential components, such as public and private keys, peer-to-peer transactions, and how Bitcoin fits the definition of a digital currency. However, Bitcoin (BTC) would not exist if its underlying technology did not exist. When they advocated utilizing blockchain technology as a mechanism to publicly verify transactions, Satoshi Nakamoto fundamentally altered the nature of the competition. Prior to that point, blockchain technology had no practical applications.

The terms blockchain, mining, trade, and wallet all came up. It's almost as if the world of Bitcoin and cryptocurrency has its own secret lexicon. In this chapter, we will concentrate on the processes that made it possible for BTC to exist, and we will continue to clarify its terminology as it is introduced.

Chain of blocks

A database is a digital system that saves information and in 1991, someone first established the blockchain. Databases may be as simple as a list with phone numbers on it or as intricate as cloud software that combines data with algorithms to maximize the information contained inside it. When it comes to blockchain, the data is not saved in a "list," but rather as blocks of information that add up to each other to present a chronological register of all the data it possesses. This register displays the data in the order in which they were added to the blockchain.

Each each block that makes up a blockchain has a certain amount of space for storing data. When that block has been completely populated with information, a subsequent block will connect to it and begin populating itself with data. Each each block in a blockchain may be thought of as its own database. Imagine a railroad, with each car representing a different piece of information. When a car is filled, another car is added to the train, and this process continues until all of the information is placed onto our blockchain railway. The information is heaped into a car and joined to the train.

It is important to keep in mind that blockchain technology is not exclusive to cryptocurrencies and that it may be used to serve a variety of functions and purposes. However, the Bitcoinblockchain technology can be broken down into its component parts in order to better understand what makes it tick. The data that is kept in each block cannot be deleted and cannot be undone. This is the first important feature. Because Bitcoin is a public and decentralized system, this is the case. Every block stores all of the information without running the danger of losing any of it and also carries a date that indicates when it was created. But just what type of data is stored on a blockchain for Bitcoin? It records every transaction that has been carried out up to the point when the blockchain's storage capacity is exhausted. One challenging element of decentralized coins that make use of this technology is the aforementioned issue. BTC is not owned by anybody. They are in possession of the particular private key that serves as evidence that the coin was successfully transferred to them. But Bitcoin is not located anywhere, not even when it is ostensibly "stored" in digital wallets.

It is imperative that we do not lose sight of the fact that even information that is kept "in the cloud" is still physically located someplace. Companies that provide cloud services often have enormous data centers, which may be located in a number of different cities and countries. These data centers house the enormous computers that store our information. Consider Google Drive and Salesforce as two examples of private organizations who own and operate this kind of storage and charge their customers for access to the databases they maintain. However, Bitcoin Core does not save its data in this fashion. There is no company called Bitcoin Inc. that owns a large tract of land in Utah and uses it as a storage facility for all of the bitcoins. BTC was designed to operate without a central administration right from the start. This concept of decentralization applies not just to the political sphere, but also to the technical sphere. Nodes are the collective name for the thousands of individual computers that are spread out throughout the globe and used to store Bitcoin. They are not owned by a single corporation but rather by a number of separate people. As was indicated before, given that the blockchain technology is not exclusive to Bitcoin, there is the potential for there to be blockchains that are kept by a single, anonymous individual. This is not the case at all, and doing so was a conscious decision.

These nodes have a different function altogether. Because every block in a blockchain holds the data of every transaction that has ever been done, if there were to be a failure in one of the nodes, there are hundreds of computers that can repair it. Blockchains are used in cryptocurrencies like bitcoin and ethereum. Every computer serves as a point of checkpoint reference for the information. Because of this, the data associated with Bitcoin transactions cannot be altered. It would need a major assault on thousands of machines, all of which would need to be located in various parts of the globe, in order to successfully change the data while remaining undetected. Having a personal node or using a blockchain explorer are the two methods to get access to the publicly available information, also known as the public ledger.

First Public Offering Of Coins

A technique of fundraising known as an Initial Coin Offering (ICO) involves exchanging future crypto coins for cryptocurrencies that are now in circulation. However, this is an extremely high-risk strategy for generating revenue. It is not a good idea to put money into something that you cannot afford to lose if there is any chance that you could lose it. Always keep in mind that it can be difficult to obtain the money back that you've lost in the event that the venture is unsuccessful.

In any case, an initial coin offering (ICO) is essentially the same thing as a crowd sale, which is the cryptocurrency equivalent of crowdfunding. The Initial Public Offering (IPO) is comparable to this, with the key difference being that tokens will be sold on the blockchain rather than shares of the company. It takes place before the beginning of this blockchain's operation. In addition to this, it entails either a crowdsale or a public sale of the initial quantity of a currency.

An ICO may also be referred to as an Initial Public Coin Offering (ICPO), which stands for Initial Coin Offering to the Public, or an Initial Token Offering (ITO). There are also others who refer to it as a Crypto Crowdsale. The companies that are just getting started in the blockchain industry are called BlockchainStartups.

Tokens, rather than coins, are often offered for sale by businesses that do initial coin offerings. It is important that you understand the distinction between these two. Tokens, on the other hand, are used to hold data streams that are multifarious and complicated, in contrast to coins, which are used to convey monetary value.

In a similar vein, the majority of businesses that do Initial Coin Offerings (ICOs) are constructed on a blockchain. Because of this, we cannot just evaluate them solely on the amount of money that they are worth. They need to be evaluated in light of the solutions they provide and the business models they use.

What about the "white paper" that the ICO has? Every initial coin offerings (ICO) has to have either a manifesto or a white paper. It has to describe in great depth not just how the technology works but also how the tokens are constructed. Additionally, it should explain to consumers how they may acquire and make use of such tokens.

You may utilize a white paper as a resource in order to learn more about certain founders and the work that they have done. It will reveal whether or not these entrepreneurs have genuinely given their concept any consideration at all. It will also inform you about the difficulties that it is able to address, in addition to describing how those problems can be solved.

Functioning of Initial Coin Offerings

In its most basic form, an initial coin offering functions as follows:

The company announces in a new commercial that it would soon begin selling the first coin supply of its newly created cryptocurrency.

The white paper for the company is presented to the investors, who then study it and ultimately trade ether or bitcoin for brand new currencies.

In order to cover the expenses associated with developing the technology, the firm is able to convert your ether or bitcoin into conventional fiat cash.

If all goes according to plan, the value of the new currency will increase, and the investors will end up ahead of the game.

Companies employ initial coin offerings (ICOs) because it enables them to raise capital for new blockchain projects in a quicker and less complicated manner. In addition to this, there are no borders. As a result, it is able to contact with all of the potential investors around the globe. The initial coin offering (ICO) participants often purchase some of the tokens, while the remaining tokens are held by the firm and used for operational purposes.

What are some instances of firms that have utilized initial coin offerings (ICOs) to raise funds for their projects? Bancor, for example, was able to raise $150 million in capital in a little over two and a half hours. There is also BAT, which was successful in raising 34 million dollars in much less than one minute. The third option is Tezos. In just one month, it was able to raise $232 million.

The ICO seems like it may be quite interesting. How do people earn money off of investing in it? A significant number of investors are of the opinion that the firm would have great success if it were to list on an exchange. They are prepared to cash in on this achievement by selling coins or tokens as quickly as possible in order to maximize their earnings. They don't truly have much faith in the firm the vast majority of the time. They could have some faith in the concept, but not enough to put their money and time into it for the long haul if there is little chance of making a significant profit in the near term.

The Mining Process OfCryptocurrency

Mining some bitcoin for yourself is one of the most effective methods to educate yourself on the subject. In the spirit of unadulterated teaching, here is a rundown of how to construct a very modest mining operation of your very own for cryptocurrencies.

Two Faces of the Same Coin: Cryptocurrency and Non-Fungible Tokens

When a miner successfully completes a certain number of calculations, which are needed to authenticate transactions that have been added to a particular blockchain, he or she has "mined" a cryptocurrency such as ether or bitcoin. A token amount of the desired cryptocurrency is given to the miner as compensation for their efforts. In principle, any ether or bitcoin may be exchanged for another. To put it another way, the value of my 10 Bitcoins or my 50 Ether is identical to the value of your 10 Bitcoins or your 50 Ether, and they may be exchanged for one another.

On blockchains, which are distributed databases supported by enormous networks of individual mining operations and mining pools, one-of-a-kind, unchangeable records of cryptocoins and NFTs are kept. You are going to enter a mining pool, but the water is not at all suitable for swimming in. Before continuing, do give the following disclaimer a thorough reading.

Disclaimer: If you've made it this far in the article, you are a true beginner. That is very cool. When you were younger, you probably enjoyed doing scientific projects much like this one. On the other hand, we are about to plunge into a world that is very intricate and exceedingly hazardous, one in which con artists, hucksters, and outright criminals are difficult to differentiate from one another. If you do decide to proceed with the actions that are explained below, we ask that you utilize an unused computer that you do not need for any other purpose. It should have absolutely no data on it at all—not a single bit! Only the operating system and any data that are completely irrelevant to you are included. You should NOT do these tasks on a computer that is dedicated to your company's operations. You absolutely DO NOT want to carry out these steps on a machine that has any kind of private data in any way. I just cannot emphasize this point enough. This is an instructional activity, and the first lesson is, "Protect yourself at all times."

Prerequisites in Terms of Equipment

You will need a computer that runs Windows and has a video (graphics) card that is at least adequate for this experiment. Given that this is only a scientific experiment, any machine running Windows will suffice. In this demonstration, I utilized a gaming PC with a mid-range specs that was running Windows 10 Home. (It features an Intel i7 9700 (10th Generation) processor, 48 gigabytes of random access memory (RAM), an NVIDIA 2080 Ti 11GB video card, and an 850-watt power supply.)

It is essential to note that this illustration is focused entirely on the graphics processing unit (GPU), often known as the video card. There is practically little work being done by the CPU, and very little of the RAM on the motherboard is being utilized. Because of this particular example, fully-loaded cargo flights carrying NVIDIA graphics cards are constantly being sent to destinations in Asia. (High-end graphics processing units are also very helpful for artificial intelligence and eSports. To simply assert that there is a shortage of them would be grossly understating the situation.)

Your cryptocurrency wallet is the first step.

It is a waste of time and resources to mine cryptocurrencies if there is nowhere to store them. You are going to require a cryptocurrency wallet. There are several of them in total. Although I have a preference for hardware wallets, for the sake of this exercise, we will be using Coinomi, which can be found online at coinomi.com.

The fact that Coinomi is easy to install and configure and is compatible with a wide variety of digital currencies are two of the many advantages offered by this cryptocurrency wallet. For the sake of this exercise, you should set up a new wallet in Coinomi even if you already have other wallets configured elsewhere. Download the program, and then be sure to follow the on-screen directions very carefully.

Joining a mining pool is the second step.

In the sake of keeping things simple, we will mine Ether (ETH). In order to accomplish this goal, we will be joining Ethermine, which is a fairly well-known mining pool.

You will choose the mining servers that are geographically nearest to you on this page when it comes time to setup the.bat files on your Windows computer so that mining can begin. Power is the most important factor in all of this, therefore choose a server that is geographically near to you.

Step 3: Establish a connection between your Coinomi Wallet and Ethermine.

Pro It is quite likely that you will be need to know the public IP address of the mining machine you are using. It is available at this location.

Downloading and setting up your mining software is the fourth step.

If you continue down this page, you will find a guide to downloading and configuring the Phoenix Miner software. Don't be afraid to try. In order for the mining program to function with the Ethermine pool, you will need to setup it. Be sure to pay attention and carry out the directions to the letter. After this is finished, you will be able to begin mining. (The answer is, it really is that easy.) However... you are by no means finished just yet. Take note: there is at least one version of Phoenix Miner that may be found on the open internet that is thought to be malicious software. The link that can be seen on the homepage of ethermine.org is the only one that you should put your faith in. Downloading Phoenix Miner from any other link is strictly prohibited.

Overclock and tune your graphics card in the fifth step.

Efficiency is the name of the game in mining. The cost of power is money. The ecology is harmed when electricity is wasted. Finding the right combination of speed, power, and precision is essential to profitable mining. Download MSI Afterburner and turn on your discrete graphics processing unit (GPU) if your machine has one. Be mindful that overclocking your graphics processing unit (or your central processing unit, for that matter) might very literally render your computer useless, so don't get carried away. Keep your GPU's power at no more than 70 percent at any one time, since this is a rather safe setting. You are free to leave the fan on your GPU set to auto, but if you want to play it extra safe, you should switch off the auto function, increase the fan's speed to 80%, and keep it at that setting. It will be noisy, but there will be no risk to your GPU. Do not make any changes to the settings for the core clock or the memory clock until you have further information about this. My priority right now is to ensure the security of your GPU; you will have plenty of time to wreak havoc on it later.

The sixth step is to begin mining!

Start mining ETH by opening a browser window to your mining pool, using Afterburner to monitor what's happening with your GPU, and starting Phoenix. After doing these things, you should observe what's going on with your GPU.

How To Turn A Profit Trading Cryptocurrencies

You may start trading cryptocurrencies right now with as little as a few dollars' worth of Bitcoin in your wallet. There are no broker fees, no middlemen that need to be dealt with, and not really any barriers to entrance or bureaucratic red tape either. All that is required of you is a little portion of a single Bitcoin. There is no justifiable excuse for you not to give it a go. It's a great way to get started with cryptocurrency if you can accept riking a few dollars' worth of payments.

I began my trading career with less than forty dollars' worth of bitcoin.

In the space of a few of weeks or less, I managed to work my way up to 5.5

Bitcoin, which had a value of almost $5,000 at the time. This is not to imply that trading is something that is simple or effortless. Quite the contrary! Trading and investing inherently include the possibility of incurring losses, but with the use of the appropriate tactics, such losses may be kept to a minimum. Everyone would be doing it if it were a simple and risk-free method to earn money, but the truth is that trading is none of those things. If, on the other hand, you are patient, have a good strategic thinking, and are able to investigate and understand market trends, then trading cryptocurrencies will be enjoyable for you.

The movement known as "Occupy Wall Street" is really cryptocurrency.

The Blockchain is a decentralized ledger, which means it cannot be controlled or manipulated by a single institution at any point in time. Its design makes transactions almost error proof, and it is also capable of doing a great deal more than just transferring ownership of digital currency. For example, it may be used for the transfer of real estate and shares of company, as well as smart contracts, commodities, and escrow services. This technology will very certainly alter the future of finance as we know it, democratizing financial markets while at the same time getting rid of "banksters."

When you are just beginning to dabble in the world of cryptocurrencies, the abundance of technical jargon may seem to be overpowering.

If you're just interested in trading and investing, having a basic common sense understanding of business, consumer demand, and economics is enough to give you an advantage over other traders (at least for the time being). Learning is important, but if you're just interested in trading and investing, having that understanding is enough. The majority of the current batch of traders are early adopters of cryptocurrencies, cryptocurrency "miners," programmers, and, more generally speaking, those who are more tech-savvy than business- or market-savvy.

They are focused on modest technological breakthroughs that may help develop hype for a coin in the near term. However, they do not give much thought to how the coin will exist outside of the exchange and the cryptocurrency community. You will have a significant benefit as a result of this.

Now, let's get this show on the road. First, you need get some Bitcoin.

There are some exchanges that will allow you purchase particular cryptocurrencies for USD, but it is a better idea to acquire Bitcoin first. There are some exchanges that will enable you purchase specific cryptocurrencies for USD. On any cryptocurrency exchange, if you have any Bitcoin, you may trade into and out of any other cryptocurrency that is currently available on the market. Remember that you are able to acquire Bitcoin in fractions known as Satoshis; for example, purchasing 0.005 Bitcoin would need you to purchase 500k Satoshis. The price of a single Bitcoin is currently $390 as of the time of writing this. Coinbase is often regarded as the most trusted and popular location to buy Bitcoin.com; alternatively, you might try to find an exchange that offers a USD-BTC pairing and trade dollars for bitcoins at a rate that is more favorable to you.

It is time to locate an exchange now that you have some Bitcoin in your possession.

Bittrex.com is, in my experience, the most trustworthy exchange I've come across. There are other exchanges; some of them are good, some of them are bad, and some of them have already been closed down. You may remember the controversy with Mt. Gox. Some individuals are completely dissuaded from using cryptocurrencies whenever there is news of an exchange being closed down or coin being stolen, but I see all of this as a necessary part of the process for any new market that is still in its infancy. I take heart from the fact that the majority of these "shady exchanges" have been shut down, and that their CEOs have been doxxed and sued to the brink of bankruptcy.

In the crypto world, news travels at a breakneck speed, so make sure you check new feed every day.

As long as you pay attention to what's going on in the world on Twitter, you should be able to smell smoke before there is a fire. Twitter users are discussing cryptocurrency exchanges as well as companies related to cryptocurrencies. Daily checks on Twitter and crypto forums, following relevant hash tags, and keeping up of what others are discussing might be helpful. Rumors are opportunities, information is power, and news is power. All three go hand in hand.

Trading may begin as soon as there are sufficient funds in your Bitcoin exchange account.

However, before you simply choose any cryptocurrency at random and follow their chart, I strongly advise you to conduct some research beforehand; otherwise, you will be trading without any knowledge of the market. The best approach to learn about each currency is to do some research on it, such as searching for "Cannabicoinann" - "ann" being an acronym for "announcement." This search query will take you to the official announcement post of Cannabicoin on the bitcointalk.org forum. Cannabicoin is a cryptocurrency.

A primer on trading.

The process of doing research on the market is known as "fundamental analysis." It is easier to 'correctly forecast trend' when one has the appropriate information at the appropriate time and has a grasp of how it will interact with the market. This is essentially the same as determining whether or not a cryptocurrency's price will rise or fall. You also have something called "technical analysis" to consider, in addition to "fundamental analysis." Technical analysis is also very important, but it focuses mostly on studying charts in order to identify patterns, such as the fact that once a coin reaches a specific price, it will continue to decrease in value.

After a coin has been dropped, the moment to purchase it is at its lowest price.

Why? Because those individuals who didn't cash out during the pump (also known as "bag holders") don't want to sell their currency at the bottom, when it would fetch a far lower price. It should go without saying that if the price of a currency you've bought moves fast upward, the best thing to do is cash out and put the money back into bitcoin. And if it's a good coin and you want to invest in it for the long term, you should definitely consider buying more after a price drop. Because a good coin will always increase again, it is often better to concentrate on acquiring good coin rather than making more Bitcoin. This is because Bitcoin's value is unpredictable.

A Ten-Day Interval Encompassed Within The Blue Vertical Line.

Once the mitigation has happened and an entry has been located, you accept the trade, place your stop loss above the zone, and then go on to the next zone. Both the demand and supply zones have already been designated. Because you hold for many days before the price reaches the next zone, this is a more traditional kind of swing trading.

Never confuse demand and supply with support and resistance when drawing demand and supply zones during the period of 10 days. Although you may sometimes see support and resistance indicating that there are lots of buyers and sellers, you should never forget that support and resistance only acts as creation of liquidity, and if you have drawn a support zone as demand, it might not hold because liquidity might be grabbed on the support zone, taking you out of the trade just because of this. Another important thing to keep in mind when drawing demand and supply zones during this period is that

Always keep this in mind: I have already explained the distinction between supply and demand and support and resistance; you can also watch as I draw out my supply and demand zones. If you believe that you have observed support and resistance instead of supply and demand, it is best to steer clear of the pair and look for another pair that displays supply and demand zones in a neat manner.

Once you have performed the analysis and you can't find any supply and demand, it's always better to abandon the pair, but only looking at this analysis, it still played out. This was precisely what I was talking about previously in regards to support and resistance. However, despite this fact, it is still risky for smart money traders to trade off support and resistance zones since we are aware that these zones merely serve to build liquidity.

In the previous illustration (number 9), the zone did not hold to the region of the take profit; nonetheless, if the transaction were managed well, it would almost certainly result in a profit. Take notice that the SL will be far narrower than that since we will be employing entrance confirmation on a much more condensed time frame. This is just meant to serve as an example. There is no evidence of support or opposition being drawn.

We can see that we have both a demand zone and a resistance zone drawn out by looking at example 10 from earlier; now that we have those two zones within the range of 10 days, we will go for the demand zone definitely; however, unfortunately, we discovered that the resistance zone still held before the demand zone; if it had been the case that we had both support and resistance zones within the range of 10 days, we would have ignored the pair entirely; however, as long as we still had a demand zone within the range, we

HistoryOfCryptocurrency

Long before the introduction of the first digital alternative currency, the concept of cryptocurrency was already in existence as a theoretical construct. The early proponents of cryptocurrencies shared the goal of using cutting-edge mathematics and computer scientific principle to solve what they saw to be a practical and political shortcoming of "traditional" fiat currencies. This shortcoming was seen to exist in both the practical and political realms.

Cryptocurrency's technological underpinnings may be traced back to the early 1980s, when an American cryptographer by the name of David Chaum invented a "blinding" algorithm.

This algorithm is still considered to be the most important part of today's web-based encryption protocols. The algorithm made it possible for parties to engage in "secure, unalterable information exchange," so laying the groundwork for the future transfer of electronic cash. This was often referred to as "blinded money."

By the late 1980s, Chaum had sought the assistance of a few other cryptocurrency enthusiasts in an effort to bring the idea of blindfolded money into the mainstream financial system. After relocating to the Netherlands, he established DigiCash, a corporation that produced units of cash based on the blinding algorithm with the purpose of making a profit. Importantly, the control of DigiCash was not decentralized, as is the case with Bitcoin and the majority of other modern cryptocurrencies. Instead, DigiCash itself held a monopoly on supply control, analogous to the way that central banks have a monopoly on fiat currency.

The Netherlands' central bank objected to DigiCash's plan to deal directly with individuals at first and eventually forced the company to abandon the concept. In the face of an ultimatum, DigiCash compromised by agreeing to sell only to licensed banks, severely reducing the company's potential in the market. Later on, Microoft approached DigiCah about a potentially profitable relationship that would allow early Windows users to make purchases in the currency. However, the two companies were unable to come to an agreement on the terms of the partnership, and DigiCah went bankrupt in the late 1990s.

An distinguished software engineer by the name of Wei Dai wrote a white paper on b-money, a virtual currency architecture that included many of the fundamental components of modern cryptocurrencies, around the same time.e, such a complicated method of anonymity protection and decentralization. B-money, on the other hand, was never really used as a medium of exchange.

Shortly after that, a Chaum associate by the name of Nick Szabo created and launched a cryptocurrency known as Bit Gold. This cryptocurrency was remarkable for its use of the block chain system, which is the foundation of most modern cryptocurrencies. However, Bit Gold was never successful in gaining widespread adoption, and hence, it is no longer utilized as a medium of trade.

Virtual Currencies Used Before Bitcoin

After DigiCash, the majority of research and investment in electronic financial transactions shifted to more traditional intermediaries, such as PayPal. This shift occurred despite the fact that these intermediaries are still digital. In different regions of the globe, a number of digital currency systems that are similar to DigiCash have emerged, such as Russia's WebMoney.

E-gold was the name given to the most prominent kind of virtual currency that was used in the United States in the late 1990s and early 2000s. E-gold was developed and is managed by a company with the same name that is headquartered in Florida. The primary purpose of the firm, e-gold, was to act as a purchaser of digital gold. Its clients, also known as users, send in their old jewelry, trinkets, and coins to e-gold's warehouse in exchange for "digital e-gold," which are monetary units that are denominated in ounces of gold. e-gold users may then sell their holdings to other e-gold users, cash out their holdings for actual gold, or swap their e-gold for U.S. dollars.

When it was at the height of its popularity in the middle of the 2000s, e-gold had over one million active accounts and processed over one billion dollars in transactions annually. Users of e-gold were left exposed to money loss as a result of the cryptocurrency's comparatively lax security protocol, which made it a popular target for cybercriminals and phishing scammers. And by the middle of the 2000s, a significant portion of e-gold's transaction activity was legally questionable. The company's lax approach to legal compliance made it appealing to money laundering operations as well as small-scale Ponzi schemes. The platform was subjected to an increasing level of legal pressure during the middle and late 2000s, and it eventually ceased operations in the year 2009.

It may not make much sense, but it's a fact nevertheless. If you notice that you are reluctant to add to trades that are going against you and that you would rather add to deals that are going in your favor, there is a good possibility that you are a successful trader.

"Averaging down" is a word that everyone is familiar with, but what about "averaging up"? It is a good idea to "average up" and raise the size of your position when your trade begins to show signs of profitability and breaks through a level of resistance or support that confirms your trade thesis. It is to your benefit to raise the amount that you are willing to risk in order to ride the trend now that you have accurately identified the direction in which the trade will go.

You will enjoy the benefits of maintaining this course of action.

When it comes to business, the price is the one buddy you can count on who will never tell a lie.

The lowering of standards is permissible as long as specific conditions are met. One possibility is when you have already scaled in lightly before this new entrance, and this new entry presents a risk to reward sort of scenario that is much bigger than the scenario you faced during your initial entry.

A significant portion of developing an effective trading strategy consists on tracking and capitalizing on an asset's momentum. When seen from this perspective, it makes perfect sense to increase one's exposure to positive momentum plays while simultaneously decreasing one's exposure to negative ones.

If you cut your losing plays early, there will be less pressure on your winning plays to make up for those major trading blunders. This will allow you to increase your chances of success. This is an essential aspect of every profitable and long-term trading plan. When you look at the chart of the plays you are now holding, you should make sure that you have indicated the level at which you would "average up." You should also identify the level at which you would reduce your position if the trade idea was unsuccessful.

"It's okay to be wrong more than you are right, as long as you cut your losers and add to your winners," said the wise man. "It's okay to be wrong more than you are right."

The History OfNft

Decentralization is the most important concept in cryptography. It is a kind of technology that is gradually becoming more prevalent in our day-to-day activities. And what exactly is meant by the term "decentralized technology"? The answer to that question is, to put it mildly, not always straightforward. On the other hand, we may consider it to be anything that does not have a centralized authority or a governing body. To put it another way, it is a form of technology that does not belong to a certain corporation or group but rather to the general public.

When we keep all of this in mind, it is not hard to see how the idea of NFTs might make sense within the context of the cryptocurrency industry. If you are new to the cryptocurrency sector, it is possible that you are unaware of what NFTs are.

Let's take a look back at the origin of non-fungible tokens (NFTs) and how they came into being.

When and where did NFTs first become available to the public?

We have discussed how Bitcoin was the catalyst for the growth of other cryptocurrencies. However, there was another piece of technology that arrived before Bitcoin and cleared the road for it to exist. Bitcoin is only possible because of this other piece of technology.

One may refer to this as a blockchain. The blockchain is the decentralized ledger that underpins cryptocurrencies. It would not be possible to transmit or receive money via the internet if blockchain technology did not exist.

Now, we are aware that non-fungible tokens (NFTs) have gained a lot of traction in recent years, and they are likely to play a significant role in the development of cryptocurrency in the years to come. But whence did they originate in the first place? To tell you the truth, everything began with a concept that was conceived of by a guy by the name of Nick Szabo.

Nick Szabo is an American computer scientist and cryptographer who is credited with the design of the very first smart contract. Szabo is also known as the "father" of blockchain technology. The Fermi Paradox was a board game that he developed in 1995, and it served as the basis for this particular contract.

Users of this game would be able to transmit a digital asset to another user of the game without making use of any third-party services such as banks or PayPal. You would have to transmit the digital item to an anonymous public key address in order to do this, and then you would have to cross your fingers and hope that it arrived at its destination. If it didn't make it there, you would have permanently lost your money, unless someone else gave it to them on your behalf. If that didn't happen, your money would have been gone.

The NFTs of the Present Day

When we take all of this into consideration, we can understand how Nick Szabo came up with the concept for NFTs long before crypto was even a thing. At the present time, a wide variety of non-fungible tokens (NFTs) are being implemented in a variety of businesses and initiatives all over the globe. CryptoPunks, CryptoKitties, and

Etheremon are some of the most well-known names in the NFT industry.

These are just a handful of the initiatives that have left an indelible impression on the NFT industry. There are a great deal more available, and you may locate them on websites such as Enjin. Enjin is a platform that was developed with the sole purpose of facilitating the production and trade of NFTs. It functions much like an online marketplace where a wide variety of digital assets may be bought and sold.

Because they are based on blockchain technology, these digital assets cannot be touched or seen with the naked eye. It is vital to keep in mind that these digital assets are not goods that exist in the physical world. On the other hand, there are certain non-fungible tokens (NFTs) that also have physical representations.

One example of this is Rare Bits' CryptoPunks and GigaPets.

Etheremon is another well-known NFT project that builds digital monsters on the Ethereumblockchain with the use of blockchain technology. When these monsters are sold or exchanged, there is no way to get them back since they are fully unique and may be utilized in combat; once they are gone, there is no way to replace them.

The number of people participating in NFTs seems to be steadily increasing, which indicates that the trend will likely continue. Launching their very own NFT initiatives is one of the primary ways in which many businesses are entering the industry. However, it is essential to keep in mind that investors who are unfamiliar with the operation of blockchain technology should approach these projects with caution since they may be highly difficult to grasp and hazardous.

What Exactly Is The Technology Behind The Blockchain?

A person or group going by the name Satoshi Nakamoto is credited with the invention of the blockchain technology. The fact of the matter is that nobody has any idea who or what Satoshi Nakamoto is; all we know for certain is that this individual was the driving force behind the development of blockchain technology.

The term "blockchain technology" refers to a kind of technology that enables the dissemination of digital information across many networks.

To quote Don and Alex Tapscott, who are the authors of the book "Blockchain Revolution:

In order to make it simpler for you to comprehend what bitcoin technology is and how it operates, I will use language that is as straightforward as possible.

Now let's imagine that in response to the recent spike in the number of crimes that have been committed at night in your community, the residents of your neighborhood have decided to establish a neighborhood watch program.

Then, in order to make it simpler for everyone to keep track of when they are supposed to be on duty, someone makes a decision to construct a spreadsheet that is replicated many times throughout the network of computers belonging to each homeowner in the community.

When new data is added to the spreadsheet by one user, it is replicated on all of the other users' computers so that everyone has access to the most recent version.

If a new individual comes into the area and desires to join the neighborhood watch, all that they need to do is register their intention to join the movement, download the most recent version of the spreadsheet, and then begin receiving updates on their own computer as well. This is all that is required of them.

Because at the end of everyone's shift, they had to write notes to update everyone else about their experiences on the shift- maybe they apprehended a criminal, or maybe someone came up with a brilliant suggestion to make their crime fighting move that much more effective- everything is set up in such a way that Mr. A, who lives across the street, does not need to come running to Mr. Y to ask what happened on his shift last night. This is because everything is programmed in such a way that Mr.

Nobody receives erroneous information, and if someone does decide to be dishonest and record an inaccurate version of what occurred on their shift, other members of the neighborhood watch can easily check the accounts of the other people that were on shift on the given day, and they can choose to go with the account that was supported by the largest number of people. This ensures that no one receives erroneous information.

Therefore, if four people say that a thief was captured when he was attempting to steal Mrs. Wilson's house, and six people say that the thief got away before he could be caught, but they were able to stop the theft nevertheless, then the version that was held by the majority had to be considered the most accurate account of what happened.

The operation of blockchain technology is just like this.

The data that is stored on blockchain is kept in a distributed database that is accessed peer to peer, and it is constantly being updated.

Because the information is not kept in a centralized database or location, there is no one person who is in charge of managing it. Instead, data is saved on several computers all over the globe (it is also possible for it to be stored on your computer, but we will discuss that in more detail later).

Therefore, if one person adds new information to the database, all of the other users on the network will immediately get the updated version;

there is no need for them to download anything since everything will be updated automatically.

Because I'm going to delve into this topic in more depth, it is essential that I clarify a few key concepts at this juncture so that I don't risk losing you along the road.

The nodes: The term "nodes" refers to individual computers that are part of the blockchain network. If you elect to link your own computer to the blockchain network as well, your computer will then function as a node in the network.

Cryptography is a term that refers to a system in which information is turned into a set of codes, which may be kept or transferred, but can only be understood by those who have permission to do so. These codes can be used for cryptography. Therefore, if you wanted to send a letter to someone that contained important information, for example, you might choose to encrypt it by putting it in codes, rather than in plain text. This would allow you to keep the information secret. After then, you will explain to the receiver how to decipher the codes, and they will be the only one who are capable of comprehending the information that you are attempting to convey.

A peer-to-peer or distributed network is a network of computers that enables certain folders and files to be safely shared with chosen users (remember our example of a neighborhood watch?)

Okay, let's put this behind us and move on.

The blockchain technology performs similar services to those of the internet, although with a number of important distinctions.

Because of the internet, you are able to compose an e-mail message, send it to a friend, and then that friend's inbox will be immediately updated so that they can view the message you sent them.

Now, here is where the issue lies with the internet. Every piece of information that you post to the internet is immediately saved to a huge server. Google has its own server, Yahoo does as well, as do banks, and pretty much every business in existence has a sizable data storage facility.

Direct And Indirect Commercial Exchanges, As Well As Brokers

These operate in the same manner as the currency exchange counters that are seen at airports. The only distinction is that they are completed on the internet. Their primary activity is the acquisition and disposal of various cryptocurrencies. The procedure of purchasing cryptocurrency via direct commercial exchanges is one that is quite easy to understand and uncomplicated. Visit the website of the exchange, choose the way of payment you like, enter the address of your digital wallet, complete the payment, and you will then be able to obtain your cryptocurrency coins. If you don't already have a digital wallet, several of these exchanges, like Coinbase and Circle, can even assist you in creating one so you can store your cryptocurrency. When it comes to acquiring cryptocurrencies, one of the easiest and quickest methods is to do it via a commercial exchange. Additionally, several of them let users pay using credit cards and PayPal when purchasing cryptocurrencies. However, in order to use any of these payment methods, you will be required to pay an additional charge for the privilege of doing so.

P2P markets, also known as peer-to-peer markets, are online marketplaces that bring together buyers and sellers of cryptocurrencies for the purpose of communication and commerce. The fact that transaction costs in P2P marketplaces are often rather cheap is the platform's primary selling point. The amount of liquidity in the market is what determines the price of cryptocurrencies. Because of this, consumers are able to purchase cryptocurrencies at prices that are far

lower than before. LocalBitcoins is a well-known example of a peer-to-peer (P2P) marketplace. This platform is used all over the globe by people interested in buying and selling bitcoins. LocalBitcoins is a platform that brings together buyers and sellers in the same geographic area and gives both parties the freedom to choose the method of payment they are most comfortable with.

Gift certificates and gift cards: Purchasing bitcoins via gift cards and vouchers is a simple approach to maintain one's anonymity. All that is required of you is to go to a store in person in order to purchase the voucher, which will have a unique code printed on it. After that, you will go to a certain website, where you will be required to input the code that is printed on the voucher together with the address of your digital wallet. This will cause the quantity of bitcoin coins that you requested to be sent to your wallet. One disadvantage of utilizing vouchers is that the conversion rates are much worse than those offered by banks.

Investing in cryptocurrencies using an automated teller machine (ATM) is the most discreet method available to those who value their privacy. It is also rather simple to do. The automated teller machines (ATMs) for cryptocurrencies are designed to seem identical to standard ATMs. On the other hand, they do not have any affiliation with any banks. On the other hand, they have an internet connection. To buy coins from a cryptocurrency automated teller machine, all you need to do is input the address of your digital wallet, choose the quantity of cryptocurrency coins you want to buy, and then feed the ATM with an amount of fiat money that is comparable to the number of cryptocurrency coins you wish to buy. Your digital wallet will be updated as soon as the coins have been sent. You could even obtain a printed receipt from some automated teller machines (ATMs). The sole drawback of cryptocurrency coins is that they have some of the highest exchange rates and transaction fees compared to other types of currencies.

Dash, which has one of the biggest market capitalization of any digital asset, is a cryptocurrency that is the subject of a great deal of debate despite the fact that it has one of the greatest values. with the beginning, Dash was nothing more than an additional cryptocurrency existing at a time when the internet was awash with Bitcoin imitators. Dash, on the other hand, aimed to achieve a level of success that was marginally superior to that of its rivals.

Dash was developed with the primary goal of addressing the issue of lack of anonymity in monetary transactions. Despite the many assertions to the contrary by Bitcoin's advocates, the cryptocurrency cannot be used in an anonymous manner. Bitcoin transactions are anonymous. When Bitcoin transactions are conducted, the details of the transaction, including who sent Bitcoin to whom, when it took place, and how much was exchanged, are recorded in a public ledger known as a blockchain. Bitcoin addresses, not names, social security numbers, or any other personally identifiable information, are used to identify the individuals participating in the transaction rather than any other kind of identifying information. In this respect, the Bitcoin addresses are equivalent to pseudonyms. Following a line of transactions until you reach one in which one of the participants discloses their identity, either purposefully or accidently, is one way to determine who the owner of those Bitcoin addresses is given that the blockchain as a whole is a public record. This makes it easy to conclude who owns those Bitcoin addresses. The appearance of anonymity is destroyed when sufficient effort is applied to linking names and addresses; this breaks the illusion of privacy.

To put it another way, Bitcoin transactions are not anonymous by design and may be linked back to the original user of the currency. However, it is possible to further conceal the identity of users of Bitcoin in the real world by "mixing" Bitcoin transactions in such a way that the relationship between address and person is blurred. This may be done by using many addresses. The most accurate comparison for mixing is as follows: Let's pretend that you own a dryer and inside of it are a number of shirts that are similar to one another that are bouncing about. You are able to place a shirt inside and then remove another item from the compartment. Nobody will know if your shirt was pulled out by someone else, and no one will know if your shirt was pulled out by someone else. Because your shirt has been jumbled up with a number of other shirts, there is no way to establish beyond a reasonable doubt that any particular shirt is indeed yours.

Even though there were and now are services that allow Bitcoin users to mix their coins, mixing is not a function that is built into the Bitcoin platform itself. That was modified by Dash. Mixing is an integral part of the Dash client and serves the purpose of protecting users' privacy and providing anonymity for all transactions. If a proxy service or the TOR network were used in combination with Dash transactions, then it would be feasible for such transactions to be fully untraceable.

In spite of the fact that Dash has a number of clear benefits, many detractors are wary of the cryptocurrency, and some even go so far as to label it a hoax. To comprehend the rationale behind it, one must first learn its background.

XCoin was the original moniker given to Dash when it was initially introduced to the public at the beginning of 2014. It was launched two days sooner than it was claimed to be, and during that time, 1.9 million coins were pre-mined. This means that they were brought into existence outside of the mining process that generates new bitcoin and bitcoin-related currencies like Litecoin. This is a significant topic of disagreement, and it is one of the primary reasons why some people feel Dash is a hoax.

Within the realm of cryptocurrencies, the practice of mining before to the debut of a project and beginning with a predetermined amount of coins is referred to as a "insta-mine." This specific instance of an instant mine was ostensibly a mistake, but in general, instant mines are looked down upon very negatively since a small number of individuals have the potential to amass the bulk of coins before the general public has the opportunity to purchase them. It is possible that these early holders may unjustly benefit from trading the coins on the open market by manipulating the value of the coins and holding onto them for an extended period of time. When discussing the stock market, this practice is referred to as "insider trading," and it is a criminal offense. Ripple/XRP was released with all of the possible tokens already available, and a considerable number was held by the creators. This kind of pre-mining is what turned off some cryptocurrency purists about the project.

There are differing opinions among members of the cryptocurrency community over whether or not the XCoininsta-mine was an honest mistake. According to the explanation that was provided by the primary developer, Evan Duffield, it was because there was a mistake in the source code. When one examines the history of the source code, one can see that Duffield made repeated attempts to halt the insta-mine and rescue the money by making modifications to the code. It took him a several attempts before he was finally successful, and by the time he was, roughly 10 percent of Dash's maximum coin count had already been mined. Duffield made an effort to rescue the situation by posing the possibility of reissuing the currency. The XCoin community, on the other hand, was adamantly opposed to this concept, and so, it was scrapped. After that, Duffield proposed the idea of giving coins out for free as a strategy to increase the coin's circulation and spread its popularity. Once again, the community had a different opinion. At this moment, it was determined that XCoin would be allowed to evolve naturally without any interference.

XCoin was rebranded as DarkCoin one month after it was first introduced to the public. And in 2015, it received yet another name change, this time to Dash, which is an acronym for "Digital Cash."

Is Dash a more desirable cryptocurrency than Bitcoin? There are benefits to using each currency. Being the first cryptocurrency gives Bitcoin a number of advantages, including unquestionably a higher market share and more acceptability. However, Dash is equipped with a plethora of features that are not available in Bitcoin, such as the capability to conduct quick transactions and the anonymity aspects that were previously stated.

The fact is that Dash was working very hard to become the "Bitcoin" of the future; but, its rocky start may have consigned it to disputed obscurity and prevented it from achieving its goal. The

Dash team has undertaken significant public relations efforts to promote the currency in order to combat the negative press that has been surrounding it. Additionally, the Dash wallet's user interface has been simplified in order to make it more user-friendly. At the time of writing, Dash has a market worth of $2.4 billion, although it has been losing steam recently and is no longer among the top 10 cryptocurrencies. Due to the fact that roughly half of the cryptocurrency community is wary of it, it is not in a favorable position to be utilized by online retailers, when other cryptocurrencies, such as Bitcoin, Litecoin, or Ethereum, are used more freely. This is a disadvantage for Dash. However, with the Dash team's public relations activities, this perspective might shift.

Putting Some Lies To Rest

As is the case with any technological advancement, there are some aspects that players who are either uneducated or misled fail to notice and appreciate. Fear, doubt, and uncertainty will only rise as a result of the distribution of false information, which will only slow down the advancement of these advances.

Bitcoin is against the law.

Bitcoin may not be backed by any government or other credible organization, yet despite this, it is perfectly lawful to trade in bitcoin. Bitcoin is a kind of virtual money that is now in use. Bitcoin will remain within the bounds of the law so long as its users continue to use it exclusively for legitimate purposes.

Miners have the ability to easily alter the total amount of Bitcoins that are accessible for their own profit.

Because of the way the Bitcoin algorithm works, there will never be an easy method to acquire one of these virtual currencies. Because certain criteria have to be satisfied before any transaction can be authorized, a transaction using a fake Bitcoin that does not fulfill the prerequisites will not be authorized. A procedure quite similar to this one is used by banks to counterfeit banknotes.

Bitcoin is worthless because it is not managed by a centralized authority as other currencies are.

The value of any currency is contingent on the availability of individuals who are prepared to trade it for goods or services. Bitcoin operates on the same fundamental concept as gold and the United States dollar, namely that none of these things have any intrinsic worth; rather, bitcoin is a medium of exchange.

Criminals make up the vast majority of Bitcoin users. The administration is going to put an end to it.

There is little debate about the fact that a sizeable portion of Bitcoin transactions were used to aid illicit activities, with a large portion of these transactions taking place on the shadowy underground market. Silk Road, an underground website that acts as a black market, was the location of the majority of these operations. However, as of today, that is no longer the case since Bitcoin is now accepted by over 160,000 retailers throughout the globe, and the number of merchants accepting it is still steadily increasing. It is important to note that even fictitious currencies are used in the commission of illegal acts.

This misconception originated due to the fact that Bitcoin transactions are totally private. Despite the fact that Bitcoin accounts do not have individual names, each Bitcoin address is one of a kind, and each transaction is recorded on a public ledger known as the blockchain. As a result, it is feasible to ascertain the identity of the person behind a Bitcoin transaction.

Because governments lack the ability to do so, they are unable to put an end to the Bitcoin network. This restriction is solely applicable to the imposition of taxes on bitcoin.

The value of 21 million Bitcoin in total is insufficient to make it useful for day-to-day transactions.

Bitcoin may be divided up to eight places after the decimal point. The lowest accessible unit of Bitcoin is one Satoshi, which is equal to 0.00000001 BTC. The maximum number of potential units, also known as Satoshi, in the Bitcoin system is 2,099,999,997,690,000, which is little more than 2 quadrillion. When one Bitcoin grows too large for everyday transactions, traders may simply switch to smaller units for convenience, much as how you would use pennies for tiny transactions. This is analogous to how you would use dollars for large transactions.

Hackers are able to effortlessly get into the system and take all of the Bitcoins.

There is a distinction to be made between the hacking of cryptocurrency exchanges or websites and the hacking of the blockchain itself. If malicious hackers are able to penetrate the security of an exchange, this reveals the security vulnerabilities of private enterprises. On the other hand, given that blockchain is decentralized, it is impossible for hackers to exploit this vulnerability. The United States dollar is a good example of this. It is not true that the United States dollar as a currency has been taken from its primary source only because one bank was the target of a robbery. Having said that, you should still take the appropriate safety measures, such as making your own secure wallet that you keep offline.

It's kind of like a pyramid scam, except for bitcoin.

A pyramid scheme is a game with no winners and no losers. The money that was invested in the program by late adopters resulted in enormous profits for the company's founders and early adopters. Everyone has the opportunity to make money with Bitcoin, regardless of whether they were one of the first people to invest or whether they are just starting out as investors. Due to the fact that Bitcoin is a decentralized system, there was never a single person responsible for its creation. As a result, the cryptocurrency does not have a CEO or another individual who is in charge of operations at the very top.

Bitcoin is now extinct.

Over the course of its history, Bitcoin has seen a number of "deaths." Hacking scandals and the arrest of Ross William Albrecht, creator of Silk Road, are two examples of the tactics that opponents of Bitcoin have used to discredit the cryptocurrency. However, the data don't lie, and they show that Bitcoin has managed to maintain its dominant position in terms of market value and usage in the real world.

Since 2012, individuals have been expressing their belief that it is now "too late" to invest in bitcoin. However, the actual world continues to get to this point, and the price continues to rise on a daily basis. Is this what it looks like to be a failure? And it doesn't seem to be slowing down any time soon.

Acquiring Knowledge AboutBitcoins

The blockchain technology underpins Bitcoin, a kind of digital money that operates on decentralized ledgers. It is not printed, and neither a single person nor any government is in charge of its distribution or supervision. Instead, it is produced by "miners" or "nodes" that are linked to the blockchain network and are located in different parts of the globe.

Bitcoin operates in the same manner as conventional fiat money; it can be used to buy items digitally in the same manner as U.S. dollars, British pounds, Japanese yen, and other major international currencies. Because more and more establishments are starting to use them as a form of payment, it may also be used to buy things at traditional retailers, such as bookstores and department stores.

The characteristics of Bitcoins

Because of Bitcoin's unique properties, it has recently gained legitimacy as a form of monetary exchange.

It does not have a central command: As I have just demonstrated, there is no one entity that exercises control over the Bitcoin network or prints new bitcoins. It is impossible for a single person, a group of people, or the government to make choices that would have an effect on the value of bitcoins.

It is Simple to Put Together: Anyone can get themselves a bitcoin wallet, purchase and store their bitcoins in the wallet, and then start utilizing the wallet to conduct financial transactions. When creating a conventional bank account, you are required to fill out long documents and go through onerous processes. This is not the case when starting an online banking account.

It Ensures Complete Confidentiality: Through the use of bitcoins, you are able to do business without anybody being aware of how much money you own, how much you are worth, or with whom you are conducting business.

It is Open and Disclosing: Anyone is welcome to join the network and begin mining bitcoins at their earliest convenience. Anyone can quickly understand how the system operates and how transactions are processed on the network since it is so straightforward.

There is a Rapidity to Transactions: Bitcoin transactions may be finished in a matter of seconds, unlike international wire transfers, which might take several days to reach their destination. As a result, you won't have to keep your buddy in China waiting for the money you paid him using bitcoin.

Transactions are Final: Once a transaction using bitcoins has been completed, that transaction cannot be undone. Because every transaction on the blockchain network is complete and irreversible, you will not be able to get your money back if you transmit it to another person.

Downloading news

It is common practice to neglect this aspect of calibre. The capability to download news from a wide number of different sources is already built into calibre. As of the time of this writing, 1543 sources (also known as "recipes") from all around the globe are supported. These "recipes" include both free and commercial material. Once downloaded, the material will be prepared for reading on your e-book reader if you have calibre handle your news subscriptions. This is the primary benefit of having calibre manage your news subscriptions. Nevertheless, you can still read the news straight on your computer if you want to. If you are intending to read the downloaded news on an e-book reader, it is recommended that you go into

'Preferences,' pick 'Behavior,' and adjust the 'Preferred output format' in the General choices to the format that is preferred for your e-book reader. This will ensure that the news is shown in the correct format when you read it. For the Kindle, this would be AZW3, and for the Kobo and Nook, this would be EPUB.

To access the news download scheduler, go to the top tool bar and click the 'Fetch news' option. With so many sources available, the most productive thing you can do is choose the ones you like most and configure them to download automatically at a time that is appropriate for you. You have the option of not scheduling automated downloads and instead managing the process manually if that is what you would prefer. Simply click the "Download now" option that appears after you have chosen a news source to get the article.

By clicking the disclosure triangles to the left of the language groups in the news download scheduler, you are able to expand the categories that are important to you (the ones that are written in languages that you are able to read). Look through all of the submissions to find anything that piques your attention. When you locate one, choose it and then select the check box to the right that says "Schedule for download." Otherwise, hit the "Download now" button. You have the ability to choose how often and when you would want it to download. Once the material has been downloaded, it will be converted into an e-book using the settings that you have selected for the conversion.

When you connect your e-book reader to calibre, the software will, by default, instantly transmit any news that has been downloaded to the device. If you do not want this to take place and would rather transfer the files manually, go to the "Preferences" section of the program, choose the "Behavior" category, and uncheck the box that says "Automatically send downloaded news to ebook reader." Additionally, if you want it to be given to the reader automatically, it is often a good idea to tick the 'Delete news from library when automatically sent to reader' option. This is because doing so will remove the item from the reader's library.

Explaining How Bitcoin Can Compete With Other Currencies To Become The Global Standard

With recent research indicating that the number of active Bitcoin users is expected to approach five million by 2019, the question of whether or not the cryptocurrency has the potential to become a global currency is now the subject of heated discussion in both the world of technology and the world of finance.

The most important aspect of this currency is that it makes it possible to make quick and inexpensive online payments without the need of conventional banking channels. One of the most significant obstacles that it has to overcome is the widespread consensus that Bitcoin is both safe and stable, despite the fact that, unlike other currencies, it is not regulated by any central authority. Instead, Bitcoin is designed to self-regulate, and miners generate new coins at a rate that is proportional to the rate at which they are mined. The fact that it is intentionally designed to be difficult to produce currency means that there is already a steady flow of currency being produced, which is a good development.

Bitcoin has achieved some kind of mainstream acceptance, as seen by the fact that major corporations like Microsoft, Dell, and Tesla have begun using the cryptocurrency. But transactions are not only limited to large firms; many smaller companies are now following suit; for example, you can now use Bitcoins to get flowers, pizza, or coffee.

If more retailers start accepting Bitcoin and more people become aware of the money, then people's faith in Bitcoin ought to grow along with it. However, a significant barrier prevents the currency from being widely used, and that barrier is the fact that it is not included in the exchanges. The first proposal for a Bitcoin Exchange Trading Fund was turned down by US regulators in March of 2017. This was a setback for Bitcoin, since it might have been a major turning point for the cryptocurrency but instead resulted in a decline in its value. It is difficult to see how Bitcoin can expand and become a currency that is widely accepted and used since it has not been accepted by significant institutions. This makes it difficult to see how Bitcoin can grow. Additional efforts are now being made to have Bitcoin classified, which will very certainly determine how successful these efforts are.

The use of bitcoin as a means of transportation across international borders

The phenomena of bitcoins has taken the financial and business world by storm, and it seems to have no signs of slowing down. In a world that places a premium on convenience, the majority of people would like to deal with something that is convenient and avoid too much hassle. Because Bitcoin is a kind of virtual money, it has begun to gradually replace more cumbersome conventional forms of cash, such as bank notes and currency coins. Businesses and financial institutions are running awareness campaigns to encourage their customers to switch to this mode of payment, which is advantageous in terms of both convenience and efficiency. The most significant benefit is that you are able to monitor past transactions and the exchange rate using a Bitcoin chart. The reasons listed below are some more compelling arguments in favor of include Bitcoin on your list of must-haves:

It's not true

When you are traveling, the process of exchanging money may be quite difficult and time consuming. When you are traveling to many locations, this is something to keep in mind. Carrying about a significant sum of cash is not only embarrassing but also dangerous at the same time. Bitcoins provide users with the convenience of transporting an unlimited amount of money in the form of a virtual state. Because of this, you won't have to deal with the hassle of having to keep track of many currencies, since it is common practice among traders all over the globe.

Let's take it easy

When you trade using cash, you put yourself in the position of being vulnerable to sudden shifts in the value of the underlying commodity. Because of the unfavorable exchange rates, you wind up spending a lot more money than you had planned to spend. Bitcoin is a decentralized digital currency that operates on a global scale. It has a stable value and exchange rate, and using it may save you time and money.

Because of the complex cryptography that goes into their creation, secure bitcoins are resistant to fraudulent activity. There is no evidence to suggest that anyone's personal information was hacked or leaked in any way. When you utilize the conventional method of money transfer while traveling outside of the country, you run the risk of falling into the hands of hackers who might then get access to your bank accounts. When using Bitcoin, only you will have access to your account, and only you will be able to authorize the transfer of funds into and out of it.

Impossible to reverse

If you are a seller, you have probably encountered a situation in which a customer revokes their authorization for a transaction that has already been completed. Because these transactions cannot be reversed, you are safeguarded from such an occurrence while using bitcoin. However, in order to avoid accidentally transferring your Bitcoinsto the wrong person, you need to exercise caution while dealing with them.

Useful in a pinch

Bitcoins, in contrast to traditional banks, do not need any kind of identity in order to create an account; hence, anybody may use them without the need for verification. The transactions are immediate, are not restricted by geographical borders or time zones, and do not need the completion of any paperwork on the part of the parties involved. Downloading the Bitcoin wallet and setting up an account are the only requirements for engaging in Bitcoin trading. Even if you have a negative credit history or are in debt to a bank or other financial institution, you will not be prevented from obtaining a Bitcoin account under any circumstances.

The Blockchain Explained: How Cryptocurrencies Operate And What Fuels Their Growth

As we have alluded to a few times previously in this book, cryptocurrencies are a one-of-a-kind method of holding a virtual currency that varies in value very similarly to how the value of traditional currencies such as the dollar, pound, or euro does; however, the variables that impact the value of specific cryptocurrencies vary.

Each cryptocurrency, with Bitcoin, Litecoin, and Ethereum serving as appropriate examples in this context, is very similar to a self-contained digital system. This is due to the fact that each of these systems has the capacity to determine the origin and destination of each coin that is included inside the system. For example, you can think of the movement of each coin through the cryptocurrency pipeline in the same way that you may think of the movement of water through a pipe to its final destination.

Because Bitcoins are the most well-known cryptocurrencies, it is impossible to define exactly how each cryptocurrency works because other systems, such as Ethereum, utilize Ether and Gas instead.

In light of the aforementioned, it is safe to assert that the operation of cryptocurrencies relies on three primary components: a public ledger, the processing of transactions, and mining. As an example, we will use Bitcoin since it is the most widely used and valued cryptocurrency. Each of them has had their meaning broken down for you.

Peers, or users of a network, transmit transactions to one another in the form of crypto coins using specialized cryptocurrency wallets. These wallets include specialized cryptographic keys, known as a public key and a private key, which are used to secure the transactions. Peers are the individuals who use the network. The private key is a secret key that provides users access to their wallets and the coins that are contained inside them (read more about crypto wallets). The public key is the key that is recorded on the Blockchain, which leaves a trail of where currencies began and where they went.

As was said previously, the Blockchain functions much like a ledger to keep track of all of the transactions that take place between peers. The underlying technology that makes cryptocurrenciespossible is called the blockchain. This makes it simpler to follow the origin and destination of individual currencies, and each transaction can be traced back to a public key. Because all transactions inside the Blockchain are public, the amount in each transaction is also public; this makes it easier to track the origin and destination of individual coins. However, in order to provide a higher level of protection for consumers, the system encrypts the information about the sender of the transaction.

The old monetary system is an example of what we refer to as a centralized system. Cryptocurrencies, on the other hand, do not need the involvement of a third party. This indicates that while there is not a centralized authority that can validate the presence of money in a particular wallet, the system makes use of technologies that timestamp individual transactions in order to ensure their legitimacy. The technologies used in each system are unique to themselves. The world's largest and most popular cryptocurrency, Bitcoin, employs a timestamping mechanism known as proof-of-work, which is more popularly known as mining. Ethereum, on the other hand, makes use of something known as smart contracts.

Now that we have that understanding, we need to deepen the information you have gained here by having a more in-depth conversation about the Blockchain.

The Cryptocurrency System As A Whole In A Nutshell

• A kind of decentralized digital currency that is created and distributed by people using just the resources at their disposal.

• A monetary system that is reliable and constant. For instance, there can never be more than 21,000,000 bitcoins generated in the whole world.

It Does not need the involvement of any government or financial institution in order to function.

• The price is determined by the total number of coins that have been discovered and used, which is then combined with the number of people who want to buy them.

• There are a few distinct varieties of crypto currency, with Bitcoin being the pioneering and original type.

• Has the potential to bring in a significant amount of money, but just like any other investment, it is not without risk.

THE MINERS' PART IN THE CONTINUATION OF CRYPTOCURRENCY

The creator of Bitcoin made the mining tool open source, which means that anyone may use it for no charge. On the other hand, the computers that they use are operational around the clock, seven days a week. The algorithms are quite difficult to understand, and the central processing unit is working at maximum capacity. A significant number of users have specialized computers that were built for the purpose of mining cryptocurrencies. The term "mner" refers to both the user and the computer that has been pecalized.

In order to ensure that a can is not copied in any form, the Manger (the human one) will also keep ledgers of transactions and function as an auditor. This prevents unauthorized access to the system and prevents it from wreaking havoc. They are compensated for their work by being given new cryptocurrency at the end of each week in which they successfully maintain their operation. They save their cryptocurrency in encrypted files on their own computer or another device that is kept in their possession. The items in question are referred to as wallets.